A. E. Housman
Spoken and Unspoken Love

Henry Maas

GREENWICH EXCHANGE
LONDON

Greenwich Exchange, London

A. E. Housman
Spoken and Unspoken Love
©Henry Maas 2012

First published in Great Britain in 2012
All rights reserved

Printed and bound by **imprint**digital.net
Typesetting and layout by Jude Keen Ltd., London
Tel: 020 8355 4541

Cover design by December Publications, Belfast
Tel: 028 90286559
Credit: Jack Thurgar
jackleahyportraits.blogspot.co.uk
wildcornerz.blogspot.co.uk

Greenwich Exchange Website: www.greenex.co.uk

Cataloguing in Publication Data is available
from the British Library.

Paperback ISBN: 978-1-906075-71-2
Hardback ISBN: 978-1-906075-73-6

Dedicated to
Susi

Contents

Preface

A. E. Housman's first book, *A Shropshire Lad*, was one of the most popular collections of poems in the early years of the twentieth century, and by 1922, when he published *Last Poems*, the second and only other volume produced in his lifetime, he was widely regarded as a great poet. His poetry has kept its place ever since, and a collected edition, often reprinted, appeared in 1939, three years after his death. It contained many of his finest poems, ones that he had withheld because they concern his love for another man, but his fame still rests largely on *A Shropshire Lad*. I hope the following pages will do something to persuade readers that the rest of his work is of even greater value.

Housman is an intensely personal poet; he wrote from the heart, but he would not let others see into his private world. In his first book he half-disguised his poems as the work of a Shropshire rustic. The pretence was not meant to be taken seriously, but the 'lad' became a proxy voice for some of his bitterest outbursts. He also drew a sharp line between his poetry and his occupation as a classical scholar, in which he attained an academic eminence as great as his poetic popularity. Yet the suppressed passion of his emotional life and the rigorous discipline of his work as a Latin textual critic are inseparable as sources of his poetry, and for this reason I have tried to relate it to his scholarship as well as his private life.

I offer my warm thanks to Mrs Linda Woodward, who read this book in draft and made many valuable corrections.

In quoting Housman's poems I have in general followed the text of his *Collected Poems*, but I have been greatly helped by the wonderfully erudite commentary in Archie Burnett's critical edition published in 1997, which contains everything that survives of Housman's drafts and uncompleted poems as well as all his Latin poems, comic verse and juvenilia. It has also been a great advantage to have available Richard Perceval Graves's fine biography, *A. E. Housman: The Scholar-Poet* (1979). Their work has been invaluable to me, and this book would have been much poorer, perhaps impossible, without it.

H. M.

1

The Name and Nature of Poetry

When he was seventy-four, A. E. Housman delivered the biennial Leslie Stephen lecture in the Senate House at Cambridge. He was old and unwell. He had been a professor more than half his life and could have retired, but he went on working in the university world where he felt safe and honoured.

For the lecture he was free to choose any literary subject, and had decided to speak on poetry. It was something many others could have done easily, but Housman was a perfectionist and would not give the world anything but his best. He was a classical scholar, not a literary theorist, and as the day of the lecture approached, he became painfully anxious about venturing as an amateur into territory long colonised by academic professionals. He had hesitated about accepting the invitation, and now regretted letting himself be persuaded; but having given way, he was determined to make the occasion notable.

Lecturing itself was no problem. It was his job, but he was used to addressing small scholarly audiences more or less in private. This was different. He would be facing the university and the literary worlds together, for besides being the Cambridge Professor of Latin, he was the author of *A Shropshire Lad* and a much-admired poet – at a time when poetry had a wide audience and was taken seriously. He was also, by common consent among classicists, the outstanding Latinist of his time. The double reputation did not make him a celebrity in the modern way, but it conferred great distinction and ensured that his pronouncements would receive attention.

He had finished his life's work, his five-volume edition of the Roman astrological poet Manilius, completed in 1930, and he had told the world that he would publish no more poetry. The lecture was to be his farewell, and it had to be memorable. He chose to call it *The Name and Nature of Poetry*. Literary taste had changed profoundly during his lifetime. Poetry was becoming less lyrical, more given to protest and mockery, grittier and harsher. At the same time the new orthodoxy of the Cambridge English Faculty had made the Metaphysical poets of the seventeenth century the sacred texts of English studies. Housman was scornful:

> There was a whole age of English in which the place of poetry was usurped by something very different which possessed the proper and specific name of wit: wit not in its modern sense, but as defined by Johnson, 'a combination of dissimilar images or discovery of occult resemblances in things apparently unlike'. Such discoveries are no more poetical than anagrams; such pleasure as they give is merely intellectual and is intellectually frivolous; but this was the pleasure principally sought and found by the intelligentsia of fifty years and more of the seventeenth century. Some of the writers who purveyed it to their contemporaries were, by accident, considerable poets; and though their verse was generally inharmonious, and apparently cut into lengths and tied into faggots by deaf mathematicians, some little of their poetry was beautiful and even superb. But it was not by this that they captivated and sought to captivate … their object was to startle by novelty and amuse by ingenuity a public whose one wish was to be so startled and amused. The pleasure, however luxurious, of hearing St Mary Magdalene's eyes described as

> > Two walking baths, two weeping motions,
> > Portable and compendious oceans,

> was not a poetic pleasure; and poetry, as a label for this particular commodity, is not appropriate.

The purpose of the lecture was to assert Housman's belief that 'Poetry is not the thing said but a way of saying it.' He gives examples, for instance Psalm 49:7: 'But no man may deliver his brother nor make agreement unto God for him,' of which he says: 'That is to me poetry so moving that I can hardly keep my voice steady in reading it.' He contrasts it with the Bible version: 'None of them can by any means redeem his brother, nor give to God a ransom for him,' which he can read without emotion. He worries little about the sense, and quotes Coleridge: 'Poetry gives most pleasure when only generally and not perfectly understood,' adding (on his own account): 'Meaning is of the intellect, poetry is not.' Try Shakespeare:

> Take O take those lips away
>   That so sweetly were forsworn ...

'That is nonsense', he says; 'but it is ravishing poetry.' Later he quotes Milton, 'Nymphs and shepherds, dance no more,' and asks, 'What is it that can draw tears, as I know it can, to the eyes of more readers than one? What in the world is there to cry about?' And he concludes:

> Poetry indeed seems to me more physical than intellectual. A year or two ago, in common with others, I received from America a request that I would define poetry. I replied that I could no more define poetry than a terrier can define a rat, but that I thought we both recognised the object by the symptoms which it provokes in us ... Experience has taught me, when I am shaving of a morning, to keep watch over my thoughts, because, if a line of poetry strays into my memory, my skin bristles so that the razor ceases to act.

He goes on to describe the other symptoms: a shiver down the spine, contraction of the throat and one 'which I can only describe by borrowing a phrase from one of Keats's last letters, where he writes, speaking of Fanny Brawne, "everything that reminds me of her goes through me like a spear". The seat of this emotion is the pit of the stomach.'

The poet on whom he relies most to make his point is Blake. There is the 'mysterious grandeur' of 'Hear the voice of the Bard' and the nearly meaningless 'Memory, hither come'. His trump card is the poem beginning:

> My Spectre around me night and day
> Like a wild beast guards my way;
> My Emanation far within
> Weeps incessantly for my sin.

'I am not equal', he says, 'to framing definite ideas which would match that magnificent versification and correspond to the strong tremor of unreasonable excitement which those words set up in some region deeper than the mind.'

He makes no pretence to offer a definition of poetry, but what matter? He can recognise it, talk about it, even write it without being able to define it. Housman has done so – and done it provocatively.

The 'new critics' of the English Faculty were outraged, and Housman reported one of them saying that it would take more than twelve years to undo the harm he had done in an hour. What he said also provokes questions. Why do Blake's lines have so powerful an effect on his emotions? Why is he moved to tears so much more than joy? And in his own poems, what is the reason for the unhappiness, the anger and the constant harping on death?

The answer lies in the world to which he was born. At some point in his early or mid twenties, he fell in love, but it was with another man, and one who was revolted by the mere notion. Most people in the late nineteenth century had come to think any sexual contact between men unnatural and disgusting. In 1885 the law forbidding it was extended in scope, and those convicted were detested as violently as paedophiles today. They were imprisoned, and afterwards ostracised for life. For Housman, who had grown up in a generally conventional family with the Christian values of the day, the fear of being found out was monstrous. He was steeped in Greek and Roman literature, and knew that classical civilisation had no comparable inhibitions, that earlier times in Britain had worried far less, and that there was a good deal of barely concealed homosexuality in the older universities and the public schools and among literary and artistic people in his own day. He may not have felt any personal guilt, but he could not escape his time. If he was to live and work in England – indeed if he was to be able to look his own family in the face – his only course was secrecy and silence. Thus he condemned himself to a celibate and loveless life. In his daily dealings with the world he became that accepted type, the bachelor whose passion went into his work, but in his poems the frustration, the fear of discovery and humiliation, self-loathing and bitterness that nature had made him as he was, sometimes made his disgust sound almost ludicrous:

Some can gaze and not be sick,
But I could never learn the trick.
There's this to say for blood and breath,
They give a man a taste for death.

(*Additional Poems*, XVI)

2

Bromsgrove, Oxford and London

He was christened Alfred Edward, but to the world he was A. E. Housman or Professor Housman; friends called him Housman; even when writing to his family he signed himself A. E. Housman. He was born in 1859, the eldest of seven children. Until his early twenties he was thought generally cheerful. His forebears were professional people; his father was a solicitor and had inherited money. The family lived in Worcestershire, and he went to school in Bromsgrove, a minor but respectable public school (such fine distinctions had a social importance that is hard to comprehend now) where he had the advantage of first-rate teaching in Classics, at which he excelled. He won an Oxford scholarship, and in 1877 he went up to St John's College to read 'Greats' (the four-year Classics course) and got a first in the 1879 examinations (Moderations or 'Mods') on the first part of the syllabus.

But there were troubles, and they had begun earlier. The first blow fell in 1871. His mother had been unwell; he went to stay with friends of her family, and while with them learned by a letter from his father that she had died on his twelfth birthday. 'Her death had a profound effect upon him', his brother Laurence wrote later, 'for there had been between them a deep bond of affection and understanding.' She had been a devout Christian, and it was probably her death that destroyed Alfred's religious faith.

Before long Edward Housman (Alfred's father) remarried. His second wife was his cousin Lucy Housman. She was good with the children; they became fond of her, and all would have been well had not Edward Housman taken to drink. The effect was gradual but disastrous. He neglected his work, invested foolishly and mismanaged his finances to the point of near-bankruptcy. His health went downhill, and in 1881 he suffered a stroke – a few days before Alfred's finals. With their income sharply reduced, and with several younger children still on their hands, Edward and his wife had counted on

Alfred to earn a good living and help the family through the crisis as soon as he had finished at Oxford. After his first in Mods, they had every reason to hope he would do equally well in Greats. It is not easy to imagine their feelings on hearing that he had not merely fallen short of the expected first, the passport to a good job, but had contrived to fail completely. The extent of his own disappointment and self-loathing must be even harder to guess. Humiliation and shame poisoned relations with his family, and from then on, the light-hearted young man was no more. Housman became the figure that the world later saw in his poetry, self-absorbed, brooding, oppressed. He left Oxford with no degree, no money and no prospects.

There was nothing for it but to go home, face his parents, ask them to let him stay while he read for that humblest of qualifications, a pass degree. His old Bromsgrove head master helped a little by giving him occasional work filling in for absent staff, but nothing could take away the awful truth that, far from becoming the breadwinner who would prop up the Housmans' failing fortunes, he was now merely a further burden on them, and unlikely to be any great help in the future.

No one knows what went wrong at Oxford, but there are theories. The simplest is that his failure in Greats stemmed from anxiety about his father. Another likely cause of stress was the intensity of his feeling for a friend. Moses Jackson was an engineering student, a rowing man and a declared philistine with no interest in Housman's literary and classical studies. But Housman wasted a lot of time in Jackson's cheery but less than learned company, hoping perhaps for some return of his own affection. Jackson was unresponsive, and the sterile relationship was a probable contributor to his troubles. The Greats syllabus involved extensive study of ancient history and philosophy. Housman had already embarked on a project that absorbed his time and attention. He was aiming to produce a text of the Roman poet Propertius embodying the results of modern scholarship and his own researches, and his concentration on this distracted him from the reading essential for the examinations. Perhaps he had thought he would be able to catch up in time; perhaps he simply misjudged the amount he had to do; perhaps earlier success had led him to believe that his undoubted ability would weigh with the examiners and induce them to overlook his neglect of the syllabus.

The year at home, and the pass degree that followed, qualified Housman, however modestly, to apply for work in the Civil Service, and in 1882 he took a job in the Patent Office. It was a humble clerkship with a salary that barely covered the cost of living in London, but the post had two great advantages. Jackson was already working in the same department, though in a higher grade – and Housman arranged to live in the same lodgings with him; and the work, though uninspiring, left Housman with the mental energy he needed for what he already knew was his proper *métier*: classical scholarship.

Classical studies have changed so greatly over the past century that it is worth pausing for a moment to look at what he was doing. In antiquity, when books were produced as handwritten scrolls made of parchment or papyrus, the Greek or Roman author's own copy (written by him or dictated to a secretary) was 'published' by booksellers, who employed scribes to make copies (by hand), and if a book was in demand, copies were constantly being made from copies of the original text, these copies were copied, and so on.

Books being perishable objects, the only way to preserve a text over the centuries was by constant recopying – which was done as a rule only for works which had become 'classics'. As a result, the world now possesses only a small fraction of the literary output of antiquity, and what has survived has been copied over and over again, sometimes by scribes who knew little Latin or Greek, or, even if they were well educated and knew the languages, sometimes made mistakes, misreading words, or misunderstanding abbreviated forms, missing out a letter or a word or phrase, or repeating it, misspelling, skipping a line, inserting a word from the line above, incorporating in the text marginal notes or attempted corrections made by earlier readers. Every time a manuscript is recopied most of those errors are repeated, and as likely as not further mistakes are added. Sometimes a copyist sees that something is wrong and 'corrects' it – but the 'correction' may make things worse by putting a plausible but wrong word or phrase in place of an obvious mistake, and thus concealing the error.

In these ways texts become 'corrupted', and modern knowledge of ancient literature depends on manuscripts written hundreds of years after the author's original work, copies of copies of … and consequently often garbled or mutilated in every imaginable way. As western civilisation is founded on the literature and art of antiquity, it has long been the business of scholars to make sense of those corrupt texts and get closer to what the ancients actually wrote and what they meant. The work began some seven hundred years ago, and though classical scholarship now concerns itself with ancient civilisation more broadly, the study of texts and the effort to reconstruct the precise original wording still continues. In Housman's time it was the principal – often the sole – concern of scholars.

The work is exacting. It is slow and detailed, and involves constant reference to countless authorities. It needs a thorough knowledge of all the main surviving authors, their ancient commentators and modern editors (which means of course a complete command of Greek and Latin), a powerful memory, a feel for the style and taste of (say) a poet or historian, an understanding of the materials of books, writing surfaces, pens and inks, how scribes work and the history of those manuscripts that have survived the ravages of time. This was where Housman's interest lay, and it was the study of the Latin poets that absorbed his energies throughout his London years – indeed for the rest of his life. Day after day he made his way from the Patent Office off Chancery Lane to the reading room of the British Museum, forerunner of the British Library, where the books he needed were to hand.

His life, though, was not all hard work. There were evenings in the Bayswater lodgings, where Jackson's younger brother Adalbert came to live as well, and days spent walking in the country. But a crisis was approaching, probably because Housman's affection for Moses Jackson was becoming too serious. In 1885 things came to a head. There was a scene, Housman stormed out of the house. The Jacksons were worried, and Moses wrote to Alfred's parents to ask if they had heard anything, but they knew nothing. Some days later Alfred reappeared, offering no explanation. Soon afterwards he moved to other lodgings not far off. He remained on friendly terms with the brothers, but the old life was gone.

What had happened? The only clue is in poems Alfred wrote but never published, for instance:

Because I liked you better
  Than suits a man to say,
It irked you, and I promised
  To throw the thought away.

To put the world between us
  We parted stiff and dry;
'Good-bye,' said you, 'forget me.'
  'I will, no fear', said I ...
(from *More Poems*, XXXI)

The two other verses of the poem tell no more of what happened, and there can be no certainty that the story it tells is exact, or that it is the drama of 1885 that is described, but the fact that Housman wrote it in the first person, without the assumed character of one of his country lads, makes it seem autobiographical. It may indeed describe a later rift. In 1889 Jackson went away to teach in India. When he came home three years later to marry, Housman was not invited to the wedding, and in fact did not hear of it till afterwards. None the less he saw Jackson on later visits to England, and in 1900 became godfather to his son Gerald.

Miraculously the turmoil of these years did not distract Housman from his studies. Indeed the separation from Jackson seems to have spurred him. He started contributing papers to the learned journals, and the quality of his scholarship was soon recognised and rewarded. In 1889 he was invited (a considerable honour) to join the Cambridge Philological Society, and when the Latin professorship at University College, London became vacant two years later, he was front runner for the post. His letter of application (which was supported by several leading academics of the day) contains some wonderfully revealing passages. 'I am thirty-three years of age. I entered the University of Oxford as a scholar of St John's College in 1877; in 1879 I was placed in the first class in the Honour School of Classical Moderations; in 1881 I failed to obtain honours in the Final School of Litterae Humaniores. I have since passed the examination required for the degree of B.A., and am of standing to take the degree of M.A. in the event of my appointment to a Professorship.' He understood the wisdom of the old adage, 'Never explain, never complain.'

The rise from a modest Civil Service clerkship to one of the leading academic posts in the land at a single bound was something quite exceptional, and testimony to the high standing of Housman's work. It also lifted him out of poverty – never to great wealth, but to comfort and the occasional luxury of dining out in style. Being methodical and conscientious, he took the work seriously. He was required to give weekly lectures every spring term, and there was a considerable load of supervision work, which was not inspiring as there were few students with any great ability or ambition, but the vacations, though not as spacious as at Oxford or Cambridge, where the summer break lasts for four months, were opulent in comparison with anything the Patent Office could offer.

One result of the change was that he now began seriously writing poetry. He had been doing so occasionally since he was very young, and he had done well in school and university competitions. Oxford had indeed elicited the first poem written recognisably in his individual style:

Parta Quies

Good night, ensured release,
Imperishable peace,
   Have these for yours,
While sea abides, and land,
And earth's foundations stand,
   And heaven endures.

When earth's foundations flee,
Nor sky nor land nor sea
   At all is found,
Content you, let them burn:
It is not your concern;
   Sleep on, sleep sound.

(*More Poems*, XLVIII)

The lines are distinctive: the Latin title (from Virgil, meaning 'Rest [is] won'), the Bible and Prayer Book references ('heaven, and earth, and sea' in Psalm 146), the quotation, perhaps unconscious, from Dante Gabriel Rossetti ('Imperishable peace'), the neat antithesis of lines 4–6 and 7–9, the balance of the first three and the last three lines. It is highly accomplished. More important: it is heartfelt.

During his Patent Office years Housman wrote little poetry. That now changed entirely. In *The Name and Nature of Poetry* he gave some account of the genesis of his poems:

I think that the production of poetry, in its first stage, is less an active than a passive and involuntary process ... and the experience, though pleasurable, was generally agitating and exhausting ... Having drunk a pint of beer at luncheon ... I would go out for a walk of two or three hours. As I went along, thinking of nothing in particular, looking at things around me and following the progress of the seasons, there would flow into my mind, with sudden and unaccountable emotion, sometimes a line or two of verse, sometimes a whole stanza at once, accompanied, not preceded, by a vague notion of the poem which they were destined to form part of. Then there would usually be a lull of an hour or two, then perhaps the spring would bubble up again.

He describes writing down the 'automatic' lines, leaving gaps where necessary, and hoping that another walk would help to fill them, 'but sometimes the poem had to be taken in hand and completed by the brain, which was apt to be a matter of trouble and anxiety, involving trial and disappointment, and sometimes ending in failure.'

This leisurely (though uncomfortable) process started slowly, but by 1893–4 it was producing a small, steady flow, which turned into a short-lived but intense outpouring in 1895, when he wrote or redrafted some two-thirds of the poems that make up *A Shropshire Lad*.

A poem dating from August or September 1895 (though not published till after Housman's death) gives a glimpse of what must have been an almost unbearable anxiety for him in that year. It starts:

> Oh who is that young sinner with the handcuffs on his wrists?
> And what has he been after that they groan and shake their fists?
> And wherefore is he wearing such a conscience-stricken air?
> Oh they're taking him to prison for the colour of his hair.
>
> 'Tis a shame to human nature, such a head of hair as his;
> In the good old time 'twas hanging for the colour that it is;
> Though hanging isn't bad enough and flaying would be fair
> For the nameless and abominable colour of his hair …

(from *Additional Poems*, XVIII)

Only three or four months earlier, Oscar Wilde had been sentenced to two years' hard labour for homosexual acts. He was the most successful playwright of the day – with three plays running concurrently in the West End. He was a celebrated wit and a great figure in the grander part of literary society where it mingles with the *beau monde*. His conviction was accompanied by a vicious press campaign against anyone 'aesthetic', any man who could be thought less than clearly heterosexual or celibate. Wilde himself was subjected to every possible indignity. He was yelled at in the streets outside the court, he was bankrupted, his house was seized, his possessions auctioned off, his wife and sons forced into virtual hiding. Troops of friends who had been proud to be seen in his company rushed to distance themselves. It was a great English *crise de moralité*.

In November 1894 Edward Housman, Alfred's father, died. For years he had played no great part in his son's life, or in anyone else's, beyond needing the care of his wife, but his departure from the scene, if it did nothing else, at any rate removed the anxiety that his family might be called on to support him in a helpless old age. Housman of course went home for the funeral, and stayed in order to help with the inevitable business that follows a parent's death. He had retained his old affection for an easygoing and kind-hearted father, but he gave little outward sign of grief, and it needs no psychoanalytic talk of Oedipus to explain that his loss was a relief and perhaps a liberation.

There was another event at that time which marked Housman much more deeply. It was the suicide in August 1895 of Henry Maclean, an officer cadet at the Royal Military Academy, Woolwich. He was a mere nineteen. In a lengthy note addressed to the coroner, he said: 'There is only one thing in this world that would make me thoroughly happy; that one thing I have no earthly hope of obtaining … I have absolutely ruined my own life, but I thank God that, as yet, so far as I know, I have not morally injured – or "offended," as it is called in the Bible – any one else. Now I am quite certain that I could not live another five years without doing so …' Housman saw the report in the *Standard*, and he kept the cutting to the end of his life. His response followed quickly:

Shot? So quick, so clean an ending?
   Oh that was right, lad, that was brave:
Yours was not an ill for mending,
   'Twas best to take it to the grave.

Oh you had forethought, you could reason,
   And saw your road and where it led,
And early wise and brave in season
   Put the pistol to your head.

Oh soon, and better so than later
   After long disgrace and scorn,
You shot dead the household traitor,
   The soul that should not have been born.

Right you guessed the rising morrow
   And scorned to tread the road you must:
Dust's your wages, son of sorrow,
   But men may come to worse than dust.

Souls undone, undoing others,—
    Long time since the tale began.
You would not live to wrong your brothers:
    Oh lad, you died as fits a man.

Now to your grave shall friend and stranger
    With ruth and some with envy come:
Undishonoured, clear of danger,
    Clean of guilt, pass hence and home.

Turn safe to rest, no dreams, no waking:
    And here, man, here's the wreath I've made:
'Tis not a gift that's worth the taking,
    But wear it and it will not fade.

(A Shropshire Lad, XLIV)

3

A Shropshire Lad

'A better critic than Wordsworth' was a phrase Housman once used of himself, thinking of the great poet's inability to leave the original – and usually best – versions of his early poems as he first wrote them. Wordsworth was a poor judge of his own work. Housman, who was widely read in the English poets – as well of course as the Greek and Latin authors – was a good enough judge to know that the poems he had collected by the end of 1895, most of them written that year, were too good to be left lying in his desk. But worry that they might give too much away made him cautious, and his first plan was to hide behind the imaginary figure of a Shropshire rustic (improbably called Terence Hearsay), and issue the book anonymously. ('Hearsay' has a further resonance: the courts do not admit hearsay evidence. Was Housman aware that his proposed impersonator's very name meant also that he could not be convicted on the evidence of his writings? *The Picture of Dorian Gray* had been used in the case against Wilde.) The assumed persona was not meant to be taken literally; there could be no disguising that the poems were the work of an accomplished writer, but the pretence was not entirely absurd, since they are mostly direct in language, written in simple ballad form with a dash of dialect words, and concerned with the everyday life of countrymen.

As to Shropshire, although he barely knew the county, he had often gazed on its hills from the high ground near his home in Worcestershire. As he later said, they 'were our western horizon', and the west always retained a romantic (though sometimes also menacing) glow for him. 'The Poems of Terence Hearsay' initially went to Macmillan, the leading literary publisher of the day, whose list included Tennyson, Matthew Arnold, Christina Rossetti, Hardy and Kipling. Macmillan's reader advised against acceptance, and the book went to Kegan Paul. Luckily, however, Housman first showed the poems to his old Oxford friend, A. W. Pollard, then an assistant in the department of printed books at the British Museum. Pollard urged him to change the title to *A Shropshire Lad* and let the book appear openly under his own name. Housman acted on the advice, and Kegan Paul agreed to publish it, but instead of paying the author an advance on royalties, charged him £30 as his contribution to the costs.

It is an extraordinary book. 'Terence' has largely vanished, and the 'I' of the poems is a figure of shifting shapes, sometimes a rustic who lives for drink and brawling, usually an observer or commentator (as in 'Shot? So quick, so clean an ending?'), sometimes an exhorter bracing young men's morale ('Up, lad: thews that lie and cumber/Sunlit pallets never thrive'). He loves the beauty of his countryside, but always with the awareness that he will not be there long to enjoy it. He travels to London and is homesick. His friends leave to join the army and die defending the frontiers of the Empire. Even those that stay at home are luckless and die young, the most unlucky on the gallows. There is little happiness in love, nothing lasts, and everything is headed for the grave. The prevailing mood is gloom and pity for the human condition, especially for those who feel themselves strangers in the world. 'My chief object in publishing my verses', he wrote in reply to a fan letter in 1903, 'was to give pleasure to a few young men here and there, and I am glad if they have given pleasure to you.'

Few of the poems have a title. All that distinguishes them is a roman number. Here is the best-known, headed simply 'II', and almost the only one that can be said to strike a cheerful note:

Loveliest of trees, the cherry now
Is hung with bloom along the bough,
And stands about the woodland ride
Wearing white for Eastertide.

Now, of my threescore years and ten,
Twenty will not come again,
And take from seventy years a score,
It only leaves me fifty more.

And since to look at things in bloom
Fifty springs are little room,
About the woodlands I will go
To see the cherry hung with snow.

Housman writes one unexpected and memorable phrase after another: 'hung with bloom', 'Wearing white for Eastertide', 'Fifty springs are little room', 'hung with snow'. It is the same all the way through *A Shropshire Lad*. 'When the lad for longing sighs', 'The blackbird in the coppice', 'When I was one-and-twenty'. Housman had a feel for the *mot juste*. Sometimes it came instinctively, but often he had to work for it, as in 'Bredon Hill':

> Here of a Sunday morning
>   My love and I would lie,
> And see the coloured counties ...

Housman's own account of it runs: 'When I wrote the poem I put down, just to fill up for the time, a quite ordinary adjective, which didn't satisfy me; others followed. Then, with the poem in my head, I went to bed, and dreamed, and in my dream I hit on the word "painted"; when I woke up, I saw that "painted" wouldn't do, but it gave me "coloured" as the right word.' In fact the draft of the poem shows that Housman started with 'sunny', and then tried 'pleasant', 'checkered' and 'patterned'.

Housman's regular use of four-line stanzas (fourth line rhyming with the second), varied occasionally by couplets, longer lines or different stanza forms, gives the pages a disarmingly similar look, but the simplicity and similarity are not all they seem. The metres vary subtly: extra syllables appear at the start of trochaic lines, making for ambiguity between trochee and iambus; stresses are inverted ('Loveliest of trees, the cherry now'); dactyls appear (as in 'The lads in their hundreds to Ludlow come in for the fair'), and even the *ionicus a minore* (as in XXXIV, 'The New Mistress': 'I will go where I am wanted, to a lady born and bred'). There is also plenty of variety in the subjects of the poems: the waste of youth, the pointlessness of labour, the dangers of losing one's heart, conflict between desire and fear, shame and dishonour, nostalgia for the countryside, girls' fickleness, rivals in love murdered, farewells to soldiers – and, ever present in the shadows, death and the graveyard.

The language too is more complex than it seems at first. For instance, in the poem that follows, 'the street/Where I lodge a little while' is no ordinary city street where he has taken rooms. It is the world of the living. 'Let me mind the house of dust' has 'mind' in the sense of 'remember'. Housman knew Matthew Arnold by heart, he remembered all the poetry he read, he had a profound knowledge of the Bible, the Book of Common Prayer and of course the Roman and Greek poets. All these constantly echo through his poems. Scholars started detecting them even in Housman's lifetime, and new allusions are still being identified.

XII

When I watch the living meet,
    And the moving pageant file
Warm and breathing through the street
    Where I lodge a little while,

If the heats of hate and lust   5
    In the house of flesh are strong,
Let me mind the house of dust
    Where my sojourn shall be long.

In the nation that is not
    Nothing stands that stood before;   10
There revenges are forgot,
    And the hater hates no more;

Lovers lying two and two
    Ask not whom they sleep beside,
And the bridegroom all night through   15
    Never turns him to the bride.

It is insidiously easy to skim over the lines and notice little before the last verse, but then one pauses a moment, and asks: But w*hy* are the lovers lying immobile and unaware? A glance back to verse 3 gives an answer; 'In the nation that is not'; but what does it mean? A moment's thought makes it evident that these are the dead. But what are they doing in a poem that starts with the living? Another look at the first verse, and things begin to become clear. We start with the living (the 'moving pageant' comes from Wordsworth) and end among the dead. The first and last verses stand in contrast. What about the lines in between? Verse 2 has the speaker (surely here the London professor, mindful of biblical disparagement of 'the flesh', and thinking perhaps also of Whittier's 'Breathe through the heats of our desire …/Let sense be dumb, let flesh retire'), reflecting that the 'heats of hate and lust' are strong only for the brief space he inhabits the 'house of flesh' and reminding himself that he will be long in 'the house of dust' (the phrase echoes Christina Rossetti). Then come lines 9–10 continuing the thought of lines 7–8, while the final couplet of verse 3 answers the first couplet of verse 2: The 'heats of hate' have gone and 'the hater hates no more'. But what has happened to lust? Lust, now transformed to love, has verse 4 to itself, and that is as it should be. Hatred and revenge pass into oblivion, but love does not altogether perish.

The whole poem is a chiasmus in which the outer verses answer each other, as do the inner ones. But it also has another interlocking structure. Hate and lust are paired in line 5, but the final six lines of the poem set them apart, dismissing hate in a couplet, but giving lust a whole verse, in which it is transmuted to love and given a sort of eternity.

Half a lifetime later, when the poet John Drinkwater asked Housman for permission to include some of his poems in a student anthology he was involved in editing, the reply ended with the words 'I am not anxious to draw down upon myself the fate which Horace dreaded, and suffer recitation in schools.' Housman would probably have retorted even more sharply if anyone had proposed to subject his work to the sort of picking over inflicted on 'When I watch the living meet', but perhaps he would have agreed, however reluctantly, that the pleasure which he hoped his poems might give could be increased by an understanding of their meaning and of the art with which he devised these seemingly artless things.

From the start the poem leads up to the final stanza, and the visual image of the pairs of lovers stays in the mind as vividly as Housman's words, but the words themselves contain a subtlety Housman must have relished. How does the last verse begin? Was it 'Lovers lying two by two'? No. Housman could do better: 'Lovers lying two *and* two/Ask not whom they sleep beside', which is preferable because 'by' would have repeated the main vowel sound of 'lying', which returns in 'beside', making too many internal rhymes. He always avoided the obvious.

Any poet careful with the detail of his work – and none was more careful than Housman, who insisted on the accuracy of every comma and semicolon – will give close attention to the ordering of his poems. There are sixty-three in *A Shropshire Lad*, and it is likely that Housman, with his knowledge of ancient astrology and number mysticism, was deliberate in the choice of that number. It is tempting to embark on a study of its symbolism, and to go on from there to consider the significance of other key numbers in the book, but the task is endless and must be left to others. Yet it is interesting that the midpoint of the series I–LXIII is XXXII, and there Housman, self-absorbed as he was in the mid-1890s, placed a poem about himself.

From far, from eve and morning
    And yon twelve-winded sky,
The stuff of life to knit me
    Blew hither: here am I.

Now—for a breath I tarry
    Nor yet disperse apart—
Take my hand quick and tell me,
    What have you in your heart.

Speak now, and I will answer;
    How shall I help you, say;
Ere to the wind's twelve quarters
    I take my endless way.

The vision is bleak, not unlike the existentialist's 'I am cast into the world to die.' What redeems it is love – here the love of a comrade, as Housman usually presented his feeling for Jackson. It is striking that this moment of self-presentation ('here am I') is followed by the most overt declaration of love in the book:

XXXIII

If truth in hearts that perish
    Could move the powers on high,
I think the love I bear you
    Should make you not to die.

Sure, sure, if stedfast meaning,
    If single thought could save,
The world might end tomorrow,
    You should not see the grave.

This long and sure-set liking,
    This boundless will to please,
—Oh, you should live for ever
    If there were help in these.

But now, since all is idle,
    To this lost heart be kind,
Ere to a town you journey
    Where friends are ill to find.

There is no disguising the devotion. He no longer asks for love, only kindness. It is abject, but it evokes pity; he can no more be scorned than Catullus, who nearly two thousand years before had experienced the same despair. Housman said as much in the other poems in this central group, in no. XXXI, 'On Wenlock Edge the wood's in trouble':

Then, 'twas before my time, the Roman
    At yonder heaving hill would stare:
The blood that warms an English yeoman,
    The thoughts that hurt him, they were there.

Poem XXX is perhaps the one that most eloquently expresses Housman's sense of a divided self:

Others, I am not the first,
Have willed more mischief than they durst:
If in the breathless night I too
Shiver now, 'tis nothing new.

More than I, if truth were told,
Have stood and sweated hot and cold,
And through their reins in ice and fire
Fear contended with desire.

Agued once like me were they,
But I like them shall win my way
Lastly to the bed of mould
Where there's neither heat nor cold.

But from my grave across my brow
Plays no wind of healing now,
And fire and ice within me fight
Beneath the suffocating night.

Taken together, the poems of this group reveal such intensity of feeling that it seems amazing now that Housman felt able to publish them. There is no explicit admission of homosexual desire, of course, and most readers a hundred years ago, knowing little about him, would not have been able to distinguish the personal content of *A Shropshire Lad* from the kind of dramatic monologue and first-person narrative familiar in ballad poetry. Besides, in those pre-Freudian days, intense friendships between men (and women even more so) were not automatically assumed to have a sexual content. Housman must simply have decided to let readers think what they liked. His professional reputation was high, his personal and social life – what there was of it – respectable, and that was an end of the matter. The likelihood must be that he confided in no one. Perhaps he even took some pleasure in the thought that he could hint freely in his poems but still keep everything that mattered secretly in his heart.

Shortly before he was sixteen, Housman had a few days' holiday in London, and dutifully wrote home to give his stepmother an account of all he had done. He visited the British Museum, the Houses of Parliament, Westminster Abbey, St Paul's, the Mansion House and Guildhall; he admired Regent Street, Trafalgar Square and Pall Mall, and heard a performance of *The Creation* in the Albert Hall, but the experience that most impressed him was the sight of the Grenadier Guards and 1st Life Guards in St James's Park. It was an interest that remained with him and was reinforced when his younger brother Herbert gave up his medical studies to join the army. Soldiers march through the pages of *A Shropshire Lad*. The first poem in the book, entitled '1887' (but written six or seven years later), celebrates Queen Victoria's Golden Jubilee by commemorating Shropshire men killed in wars to defend the empire:

... Lads, we'll remember friends of ours
  Who shared the work with God.

To skies that knit their heartstrings right,
    To fields that bred them brave,
The saviours come not home to-night;
    Themselves they could not save.

It dawns in Asia, tombstones show
    And Shropshire names are read;
And the Nile spills his overflow
    Beside the Severn's dead.

The imperial note is uncomfortable now, especially when coupled with
the assertion that defending the Empire is doing God's work, but it
sounded constantly in late Victorian poetry, and the life of the common
soldier had become a popular subject with the success of Kipling's
Barrack Room Ballads in 1892. Housman adds a touch of sentimentality
to Kipling's realism when the army poems become personal:

XXII

The street sounds to the soldiers' tread,
    And out we troop to see:
A single redcoat turns his head,
    He turns and looks at me.

My man, from sky to sky's so far,
    We never crossed before;
Such leagues apart the world's ends are,
    We're like to meet no more;

What thoughts at heart have you and I
    We cannot stop to tell;
But dead or living, drunk or dry,
    Soldier, I wish you well.

Occasional mawkishness is a fault in Housman, but rare, even in
proportion to the small corpus of his poetry. More often he is grimly
realistic about army life; the pointless waste of young men saddens
and angers him (long before the poets of the First World War made
it their stock-in-trade), most effectively perhaps in these lines from
poem XXXV, 'On the idle hill of summer':

Far and near and low and louder
    On the roads of earth go by,
Dear to friends and food for powder,
    Soldiers marching, all to die.

East and west on fields forgotten
    Bleach the bones of comrades slain,
Lovely lads and dead and rotten;
    None that go return again.

Certainly there is no sentimentality or stupid militarism here. Other subjects, though less prominent, evoke stronger feeling, particularly a sharp nostalgia for the countryside of his early years, most famously here:

XL

Into my heart an air that kills
    From yon far country blows:
What are those blue remembered hills,
    What spires, what farms are those?

That is the land of lost content,
    I see it shining plain,
The happy highways where I went
    And cannot come again.

Likewise in poem L ('In valleys of springs of river'):

By bridges that Thames runs under
    In London, the town built ill,
'Tis sure small matter for wonder
    If sorrow is with one still.

The poem ends with two of the saddest stanzas Housman wrote. Although he was by no means always depressed (he had a lighter side and could enjoy the conviviality of university life more heartily than his poetry would ever make a reader think), there were times when the contemplation of a life without love (not only Jackson's rejection but the impossibility for a man in his situation ever to declare himself) made him wish it could be over:

Where shall one halt to deliver
The luggage I'd lief set down?
Not Thames, nor Teme is the river,
Nor London nor Knighton the town:

'Tis a long way further than Knighton,
A quieter place than Clun,
Where doomsday may thunder and lighten
And little 'twill matter to one.

The hopelessness is not unlike that of Hardy's Jude. Housman admired Hardy (whom he later met and liked). They shared the *mal de siècle*, the feeling of life's pointlessness, that pervades much of the literature and art of the late nineteenth century.

With Hardy he also shared a fascination with death by hanging. As as a boy Hardy had seen a woman hanged, and the memory never left him. Public executions ended in 1868, but the gallows remained a macabre image in many people's minds for long after. Certainly they haunted Housman:

They hang us now in Shrewsbury jail:
The whistles blow forlorn,
And trains all night groan on the rail
To men that die at morn.

There sleeps in Shrewsbury jail to-night,
Or wakes, as may betide,
A better lad, if things went right,
Than most that sleep outside.   (from *A Shropshire Lad*, IX)

Precision is one of Housman's great merits. The prison in Shrewsbury is near the railway line. 'Groan' is the exact word for the sound of the London trains crossing the bridge and rounding the curve just outside the station. There is sharp observation here. It is not the kind of information to be got from a guidebook.

Although *A Shropshire Lad* was published in the 1890s, it shares little of the aestheticism of poets like Yeats and Dowson, Wilde (before he wrote *The Ballad of Reading Gaol*) and Arthur Symons, whose great concern was with beauty of image and sound. Housman's excellence is in diction, in the compression of language symbolising the compression of emotion. He is not a poet for the schoolroom, and though a poem like this can be appreciated as a collocation of beautiful sounds, most of his work is highly disciplined and cannot be enjoyed aright without careful attention. But there is no escaping one's time, and in *A Shropshire Lad* there are poems that belong unmistakably to the period, most memorably poem LIV, a pastoral elegy for the friends of his youth:

LIV

With rue my heart is laden
　For golden friends I had,
For many a rose-lipt maiden
　And many a lightfoot lad.

By brooks too broad for leaping
　The lightfoot lads are laid;
The rose-lipt girls are sleeping
　In fields where roses fade.

The vowel patterning, the close attention to the weight of the words or length of syllables, and their power to speed or slow a line, proclaim that this is an 1890s poem as clearly as a date added at the end. The long and mostly diphthongal vowels of the opening lines (in 'rue', 'my', 'laden', 'golden') toll like a bell for the dead; the alliterations, delayed till the fourth line, intensify through the rest of the poem to sharpen the *desiderium*, the pain of longing for friends who will not return.

Housman once remarked that however technically correct it might be to regard him as a poet of the Nineties, it was inappropriate, but a poem like this is clear evidence that if he had chosen to follow the favoured style of the day he would have become one of its leaders. Perhaps it was later an advantage that his poems were untainted by the 'decadence', the indoor atmosphere of the city, heavy with the faded flowers of late aestheticism. English poetic fashion changed quickly in the years that followed, and Housman then came to be seen as a poet of the open air, the countryside and that emblem of British manliness, beer. Housman (as he mentions in the Leslie Stephen lecture) drank it as a matter of course, and it turns up now and then in *A Shropshire Lad*, usually as an antidote to gloom:

Oh I have been to Ludlow fair
And left my necktie God knows where,
And carried half-way home, or near,
Pints and quarts of Ludlow beer;
Then the world seemed none so bad,
And I myself a sterling lad;

– and, also from LXII, the penultimate poem:

Why, if 'tis dancing you would be,
There's brisker pipes than poetry.
Say, for what were hop-yards meant,
Or why was Burton built on Trent?
Oh many a peer of England brews
Livelier liquor than the Muse,
And malt does more than Milton can
To justify God's ways to man.

The great merit of beer in *A Shropshire Lad* is that it stops a man thinking:

XLIX

Think no more, lad, laugh, be jolly:
    Why should men make haste to die?
Empty heads and tongues a-talking
Make the rough road easy walking,
And the feather pate of folly
    Bears the falling sky.

Oh, 'tis jesting, dancing, drinking
    Spins the heavy world around.
If young hearts were not so clever,
Oh, they would be young for ever:
Think no more; 'tis only thinking
    Lays lads underground.

The moods shift; so, sometimes, does the style. But the man behind the poems does not change. *A Shropshire Lad* reveals by no means all of him. Disappointed love, though we are given glimpses of it, hardly appears in its true guise. There are other sides of Housman (not things that needed to kept secret) which would have been out of place in the book. Like the man in Boswell who said, 'I have tried too in my time to be a philosopher; but, I don't know how, cheerfulness was always breaking in,' Housman among friends was good company, by no means the old misery for whom 'Terence' was the improbable *persona*, but the poems he chose to publish in 1896 formed a unified book, and it is right to end this account of it as he chose to end it:

LXIII

I hoed and trenched and weeded,
   And took the flowers to fair:
I brought them home unheeded;
   The hue was not the wear.

So up and down I sow them
   For lads like me to find,
When I shall lie below them,
   A dead man out of mind.

Some seed the birds devour,
   And some the season mars,
But here and there will flower
   The solitary stars,

And fields will yearly bear them
   As light-leaved spring comes on,
And luckless lads will wear them
   When I am dead and gone.

4

The Favour of Fortune

A Shropshire Lad appeared in March 1896. It was mostly well reviewed, but respectfully rather than with great enthusiasm The best notice appeared in the *New Age*, where Hubert Bland wrote of the 'distinctively new poetry … it says and sings things that have not been sung or said before, and this with a power of directness, and with a heart-penetrating quality for which one may seek in vain through the work of any contemporary lyrist.' But one excellent review was not enough to boost sales, and Housman did not, like Byron, wake up to find himself famous. Gradually, however, the book gained a small, discerning body of readers. In December Housman was sitting at dinner next to the Professor of Greek at Liverpool, G. H. Rendall, who was interested to learn that he was a brother of Laurence Housman, of whose *Green Arras* he said, 'I think it is the best volume by him that I have seen: the *Shropshire Lad* had a pretty cover.' Housman relayed the remark to Laurence. He closed the letter with 'I remain, Your affectionate brother (what a thing is fraternal affection that it will stand these tests!)', adding as a postscript, 'I was just licking the envelope when I thought of the following venomed dart: I had far, far rather that people should attribute my verses to you than yours to me.'

Among those who realised the quality of Housman's poems was Grant Richards, then just about to set up as a publisher. In October 1896 he wrote to Housman offering to publish the successor to *A Shropshire Lad*. Housman put him off, but Richards did not give up easily, and failing to get a new book of poems out of Housman, he proposed a second edition of *A Shropshire Lad*, which duly appeared in 1898. Richards was much more energetic than Kegan Paul in promoting the book. Sales took time to pick up, but Richards was sure it would establish itself and continued to reprint it. The outbreak of the Boer War in 1899 increased the popularity of military poetry, and it helped that several of Housman's poems were about soldiers. Another form in which *A Shropshire Lad* gained a wider audience was through music. Composers, always on the lookout for new poems to set, soon saw in Housman's straightforward, simple style and emotional intensity an excellent vehicle for their compositions. The most notable among them was Vaughan Williams, whose song cycle *On Wenlock Edge* appeared in 1909 and remains in the repertoire.

Housman also began meeting other writers, sometimes in the company of Richards, with whom he shared a growing fondness for *haute cuisine*. The income from his professorship enabled him to travel, and he started taking his holidays abroad, usually in France and Italy. The classical papers which he had been producing regularly since the 1880s continued to appear, and he began work on the task that was to occupy him till he was past seventy, a scholarly edition of the minor Roman poet Manilius, published in five volumes, from 1903 to 1930.

'I adjure you not to waste your time on Manilius,' Housman wrote to Robert Bridges in 1924. 'He writes on astronomy and astrology without knowing either. My interest is purely technical.' Why should a scholar of Housman's distinction have spent a great part of his life working on a poet not worth reading? It has long been a difficulty for any classicist wishing to excel in textual criticism that over the centuries since the early Renaissance some of the acutest minds in Europe (and later in America) have been engaged on the same task. The emphasis was naturally always on the great figures of Greek and Roman literature, with the result that by Housman's time there was little scope for any major work on the famous writers.

For Housman the choice of Manilius for his *magnum opus* had a double attraction. He had been interested in astronomy since he was a boy; and (far more important) the only two earlier editions had been the work of two of the greatest of scholars, Joseph Justus Scaliger in the sixteenth century and Richard Bentley in the eighteenth. It was bold to set oneself alongside them, but great advances had been made since Bentley's day, even in such simple matters as ease of travel (essential for examining manuscripts in foreign libraries) and the use of photography for facsimiles of manuscripts otherwise inaccessible. More important, the nineteenth century had seen the development of new methods of criticism which put the whole process on a more rational footing and made it less dependent on guesswork. There was room for a new edition, and Housman, already, in his early forties, among the foremost Latinists of the day, was eminently qualified to undertake it.

When the first volume was published (by Richards, but at Housman's expense) in 1903, it bore a Latin dedication to Moses Jackson, 'my comrade, who cares nothing for books like this'. Jackson had never pretended to take any interest in literature, and the form of the dedication almost overtly declares Housman's disappointment that the friend, to whom he was offering this gift of a lifetime's labour, had no notion of its value. Dedications of this sort were traditionally written in the third person ('Dedicated by the author to *his* friend …'). It is a mark of strong feeling that Housman disregarded convention and wrote '*my* comrade'. The twenty-eight-line Latin dedicatory poem that follows is formal, but becomes openly personal when Housman says: 'I do not importune the immortal gods, but, smitten with the love of noble character, it is with human aid that I choose to seek fame. A man myself, I have chosen a man, one who is strong and was for a brief span my comrade, one who has allowed his name to stand at the head of my book.'

Jackson, far away in India, received a copy, but if he ever opened it, he would not have come near to comprehending the passion in the marmoreal Latin of its dedication. Even to fellow scholars its full sense would be intelligible only if they knew Housman well and could imagine the desolate world in which he wrote the lines. He never told his love in English as he did here in Latin in the opening volume of the work that was to be his monument.

Housman's admiration for the great scholars of the past, though never uncritical, was as fervent as the devotion of pious worshippers to the saints. But it was matched by the ferocity of his scorn for editors who were not up to the mark. There was no mercy in his soul for them. He denounced them with the savagery of a man enraged by an irremediable injustice. As it was done humorously, readers can enjoy the fun, but there is no concealing the obsessive fury of the abuse hurled here (and in other prefaces and articles) at scholars guilty of no crime more odious than incompetence. Here is an example: ' … Elias Stoeber, whose reprint of Bentley's text, with a commentary designed to confute it, saw the light in 1767 at Strasburg, a city still famous for its geese … Stoeber's mind, though that is no name to call it by, was one which turned as unerringly to the false, the meaningless, the unmetrical, and the ungrammatical, as the needle to the pole.' And a few pages further on, mocking the obviously unsatisfactory critical method of sticking to a 'best' manuscript through thick and thin and adopting its readings, no matter how corrupt:

An editor of no judgment, perpetually confronted with a couple of MSS to choose from, cannot but feel in every fibre of his being that he is a donkey between two bundles of hay. What shall he do now? Leave criticism to critics, you may say, and betake himself to any honest human trade for which he is less unfit. But he prefers a more flattering solution: he confusedly imagines that if one bundle of hay is removed he will cease to be a donkey.

Housman sometimes even indulged this vindictiveness, so to speak, in advance, jotting down in a notebook, as he thought of them, insults ready for use when he found victims – for instance: 'I can easily understand why Mr — should not tell the truth about other people. He fears reprisals: he apprehends that they may tell the truth about him'; and 'When — has acquired a scrap of misinformation he cannot rest till he has imparted it.'

This is not amiable fun, but at any rate it is kept for professional polemics. Yet fun it is, and it is evidence that, besides Housman the profound but crusty scholar, and Housman the gloomy poet of unrequited love and early death, there is a third literary Housman, a cousin perhaps of the *bon viveur* and travelling *milord*: a man whose habitual depression was punctuated by hilarity, who wrote nonsense verse, as good as the best of Belloc or Lewis Carroll, merely for the amusement of friends and family:

When Adam day by day
  Woke up in Paradise,
He always used to say
  'Oh, this is very nice.'

But Eve from scenes of bliss
  Transported him for life.
The more I think of this
  The more I beat my wife.

And

I knew a Cappadocian
  Who fell into the Ocean:
His mother came and took him out
  With tokens of emotion.

She also had a daughter
Who fell into the Water:
At any rate she would have fallen
If someone hadn't caught her.

The second son went frantic
And fell in the Atlantic:
His parent reached the spot too late
To check her offspring's antic.

Her grief was then terrific:
She fell in the Pacific,
Exclaiming with her latest breath
'I have been too prolific.'

One more – if only because it is less well known, though it is one of
the most ingenious:

It is a fearful thing to be
The Pope.
That cross will not be laid on me,
I hope.
A righteous God would not permit
It.
The Pope himself must often say,
After the labours of the day,
'It is a fearful thing to be
Me.'

In 1910 the Latin professorship at Cambridge became vacant, and
Housman was asked to let his name go forward as a candidate. There
were others standing, and the vituperative tone he adopted in his
controversial writing, in contempt of the customary academic
courtesies, had made him enemies, but the electors decided he was
their man, dispensed with the usual procedure of trial lectures and
simply gave the appointment to Housman, who also became a Fellow
of Trinity College. He was at the top of the profession.

5

Last Poems

Manilius was a long haul. The second of the five books did not come out until 1912, nine years after the first. The less exacting duties of the Cambridge professorship left more leisure, and the great work speeded up. The next volume appeared in 1916, followed by the fourth in 1920. It was twenty-four years by then since *A Shropshire Lad*, years in which it had become a best-seller, probably the most successful book of poems by a single author at the time, and people sometimes asked when its successor was coming. One man who was particularly interested in the prospect of more poetry from Housman was his publisher. *A Shropshire Lad* was a fixture in Grant Richards's list, and had made a considerable contribution to the often shaky fortunes of his firm, all the more so since Housman refused royalties on the book, asking instead that his share of the profits should be used to reduce the price. But as for a successor, there seemed to be no prospect of one. Some years Housman wrote a poem or two, occasionally a few more, but often there were none at all. Yet in 1920 he started to think about a new volume. He asked Richards how long it would take to bring out a (very hypothetical) book of poems, and he started a fresh notebook in which he entered fair copies of new pieces and revisions and completed versions of ones begun earlier, but nothing more happened until 1922.

Housman's sixty-third birthday fell on 26 March that year. He had passed the grand climacteric, the sixty-third year of life which ancient astrologers believed to be a time of crisis and great change (sixty-three was the number of poems in *A Shropshire Lad*, quite possibly chosen for its symbolism). The astrologers were right, but it was probably not till after his birthday that he learned that Moses Jackson was ill (with stomach cancer) and did not have long to live.

Jackson had retired from teaching in India in 1911 and settled in British Columbia, where he bought a farm. Housman still loved him, perhaps still hoped for some kind of reunion, and now had to accept that it would never happen. Four days after his birthday he wrote his *requiescat* for his friend, 'Wake not for the world-heard thunder' with its memorable last verse:

> Sleep, my lad: the French are landed,
>> London's burning, Windsor's down;
> Clasp your cloak of earth about you,
> We must man the ditch without you,
> March unled and fight short-handed,
>> Charge to fall and swim to drown.
> Duty, friendship, bravery o'er,
> Sleep away, lad; wake no more.

(from *Last Poems*, XXIX)

The news of Jackson's illness released the springs that seemed to have dried to a mere trickle all those years. In the next ten days Housman wrote a further six poems and filled some fifty pages of his notebook with completed versions and revisions of ones begun earlier. As early as 9 April he wrote to tell Richards that he would almost certainly have a new volume ready for publication in the autumn, and in mid-June he sent the manuscript. The speed with which he worked makes it likely that he wanted the book to appear in time for Jackson to see it, but he was as careful as ever with the selection and arrangement of the poems. Housman was very definite in his judgement of other people's poetry but less sure about his own and wanted to consult friends whose opinion he respected. Accordingly the poems were initially printed on separate pages arranged at first only by their various metres, so that he would be able to settle the final order once he had definitely decided which were to be included. This caused delays, but the book was still ready for publication on 19 October.

Richards had announced it four weeks earlier, and the news had stirred up interest. There was a leading article as well as a review in *The Times* on 17 October, almost every other paper carried enthusiastic notices, and before the end of the year Richards had printed over 20,000 copies. It was in any case a good year in English literature, marked with a volume by Hardy, Joyce's *Ulysses* and, most notably, *The Waste Land*. Richards had queried the proposed title, *Last Poems*, but Housman insisted, and gave his reasons in a preface (worth reprinting here as it is omitted from the standard edition of his *Collected Poems*):

I publish these poems, few though they are, because it is not likely that I shall ever be impelled to write much more. I can no longer expect to be revisited by the continuous excitement under which in the early months of 1895 I wrote the greater part of my other book, nor indeed could I well sustain it if it came; and it is best that what I have written should be printed while I am here to see it through the press and control its spelling and punctuation. About a quarter of the matter belongs to the April of the present year, but most of it dates between 1895 and 1910.

September 1922

'Few though they are …': Housman pared down the final number to forty-one – not counting the prefatory poem, because it is a translation. The number of poems in Horace's *Odes* plus the *Carmen saeculare* was 104, and perhaps he liked the thought that his own total (forty-one added to the sixty-three of *A Shropshire Lad*) was the same.

But none of this mattered in comparison with getting the book to Jackson in time for him to read it, and perhaps for once to understand Housman's devotion. Jackson's copy went off on publication day with a letter, mostly in tones of undergraduate mock-boasting: 'The cheerful and exhilarating tone of my verse is so notorious that I feel sure it will do you more good than the doctors, though you do not know, and there are no means of driving the knowledge into your thick head, what a bloody good poet I am.' Housman goes on with news of the sales and reviews, and the fame of *A Shropshire Lad*, and ends the long paragraph (which is followed only by a few lines of trivia) with: 'Please to realise therefore, with fear and respect, that I am an eminent bloke, though I would much rather have followed you round the world and blacked your boots.' He had spoken his love at last. Jackson had time to read the book, but he was already in hospital and died on 14 January 1923.

*　*　*

They say my verse is sad; no wonder;
　Its narrow measure spans
Tears of eternity, and sorrow,
　Not mine, but man's.   (*More Poems*, prefatory poem)

The lines date from soon after the appearance of *A Shropshire Lad* , but they are not in *Last Poems*. The book is the work of an older, man, who has lived through the Great War and shared the sorrow of others at the loss of loved ones, among them his own nephew, killed in France in 1915. Even when young, he had taken a gloomy view of the world. By 1922 his mood had darkened further. The war had finally proved what he had always known: that the world is cruel and its hopes illusions. Age and eminence emboldened him to say so more openly and to publish poems too dangerous for 1896.

> The laws of God, the laws of man,
> He may keep that will and can;
> Not I; let God and man decree
> Laws for themselves and not for me;
> And if my ways are not as theirs
> Let them mind their own affairs …   (from *Last Poems*, XII)

This is not 'Terence Hearsay' speaking: it is the Kennedy Professor of Latin, the luminary of Trinity, the eminent scholar. When *Jude the Obscure* was published in 1895, Edmund Gosse, in a famous review, asked 'What has Providence done to Mr Hardy that he should arise in the arable land of Wessex and shake his fist at his Creator?' He might well have asked the same question of Housman. Gosse knew that Providence had condemned Hardy to a loveless marriage and given England divorce laws that kept him tied to his dreadful wife. He knew Housman, and must have guessed that he too lived without love and had good reason to detest a God in whose name British law made homosexual acts a crime which society did not forgive. And shake his fist is just what Housman did:

> Tell me not here, it needs not saying,
>   What tune the enchantress plays
> In aftermaths of soft September
>   Or under blanching mays,
> For she and I were long acquainted
>   And I knew all her ways …

Possess, as I possessed a season,
    The countries I resign,
Where over elmy plains the highway
    Would mount the hills and shine,
And full of shade the pillared forest
    Would murmur and be mine.

For nature, heartless, witless nature,
    Will neither care nor know
What stranger's feet may find the meadow
    And trespass there and go,
Nor ask amid the dews of morning
    If they are mine or no.   (from *Last Poems*, XL)

Clad only for form's sake in the vestments of the rustic, Housman once at least, allows himself a bitter attack on God himself:

The chestnut casts his flambeaux, and the flowers
    Stream from the hawthorn on the wind away,
The doors clap to, the pane is blind with showers,
    Pass me the can, lad; there's an end of May.

There's one spoilt spring to scant our mortal lot,
    One season ruined of our little store.
May will be fine next year as like as not:
    Oh ay, but then we shall be twenty-four.

We of a certainty are not the first
    Have sat in taverns while the tempest hurled
Their hopeful plans to emptiness, and cursed
    Whatever brute and blackguard made the world.

*   *   *

The troubles of our proud and angry dust
    Are from eternity, and shall not fail.
Bear them we can, and if we can we must.
    Shoulder the sky, my lad, and drink your ale.

(from *Last Poems*, IX)

This sounds a note hardly heard in *A Shropshire Lad*. Housman started the poem in 1895 and added to it occasionally over the years, but wrote the concluding stanza only in April 1922 when the tranquillity of of his Cambridge life was broken by the news about Jackson. His rage at the 'brute and blackguard' responsible for the world's misery could hardly have been given such violent expression before the Great War.

The stoicism with which Housman ends the poem – as if a pint or two could really make misery bearable – appears in nobler form in 'The Oracles'. The ancient Greek oracles at Dodona and Delphi speak no more, he says, but the human heart remains a true guide without the paltering half-truths which the priestess of Apollo yelled out as if the god were speaking through her. It is 480 BC, the Persians have invaded Greece with an immense army, so vast (as Herodotus reports) that when they come to a river the men drink it dry; and when the archers shoot their arrows the sun is darkened. The Spartans, posted to hold them at Thermopylae, know they are betrayed; but rather than retreat from a hopeless battle, they resolve to stand and fight, and to die as proud Greeks in their finest array. It is all done in an unforgettable last line – the response of brave men to the certainty of death:

XXV

'Tis mute, the word they went to hear on high Dodona mountain
　　When winds were in the oakenshaws and all the cauldrons tolled,
And mute's the midland navel-stone beside the singing fountain,
　　And echoes list to silence now where gods told lies of old.

I took my question to the shrine that has not ceased from speaking,
　　The heart within, that tells the truth and tells it twice as plain;
And from the cave of oracles I heard the priestess shrieking
　　That she and I should surely die and never live again.

Oh priestess, what you cry is clear, and sound good sense I think it;
　　But let the screaming echoes rest, and froth your mouth no more.
'Tis true there's better boose than brine, but he that drowns must drink it;
　　And oh, my lass, the news is news that men have heard before.

> *The King with half the East at heel is marched from lands of morning;*
> > *Their fighters drink the rivers up, their shafts benight the air.*
> *And he that stands will die for nought, and home there's no returning.*
> > The Spartans on the sea-wet rock sat down and combed their hair.

The poem was not new – it had appeared in a magazine in 1903 – but the last verse caught the mood of a country still mourning the vast losses of the Great War and ready to overlook the grim message of the earlier lines.

The War is commemorated prominently in a group of five poems early in the book (IV–VIII), and most effectively in the famous 'Epitaph on an Army of Mercenaries' (the title answers the sneer of the German press at the small British army of professional soldiers that took the field in Belgium in 1914 against all the odds to face the vast conscript German force marching to invade France):

XXXVII

These in the day when heaven was falling,
> The hour when earth's foundations fled,
Followed their mercenary calling
> And took their wages and are dead.

Their shoulders held the sky suspended;
> They stood and earth's foundations stay;
What God abandoned, these defended,
> And saved the sum of things for pay.

There is a balance here between the restrained mourning of the epitaphs in the Greek Anthology and the irony of Clough and Arnold, mixing admiration for the heroism of the 'mercenaries' with a satirical pretence of acquiescing in German scorn. There is classicism in the structure as well as in the tone, the correspondence between the first two lines of the two verses, and the echo linking their last lines.

The 'Epitaph' is the only one of the poems published by Housman that shows any marked influence of his classical studies. He himself said that the only sources he recognised in his poetry were the Scottish Border ballads, Shakespeare's songs and Heine (whose 'Armesuenderblume' he paraphrases in 'Sinner's Rue' – XXX in *Last Poems*, which ends with a characteristic verse, addressed to the suicide buried at the crossroads:

Dead clay that did me kindness,
    I can do none to you,
But only wear for breastknot
    The flower of sinner's rue.

He is mawkish here, as in an end-of-year poem, where self-pity goes too far:

XXVIII

Now dreary dawns the eastern light,
    And fall of eve is drear,
And cold the poor man lies at night,
    And so goes out the year.

Little is the luck I've had,
    And oh, 'tis comfort small
To think that many another lad
    Has had no luck at all.

But such lapses are rare in Housman. They occur in the poems where the emotion seems generalised. When he is directly engaged with the thought of a friend of flesh and blood (in the poem below, written in April 1922, it is of course Jackson), he can be superb:

XX

The night is freezing fast,
    To-morrow comes December;
        And winterfalls of old
Are with me from the past;
    And chiefly I remember
        How Dick would hate the cold.

Fall, winter, fall; for he,
    Prompt hand and headpiece clever,
        Has woven a winter robe,
And made of earth and sea
    His overcoat for ever,
        And wears the turning globe.

The poem uses a technical device unique in Housman: the six-line stanza with rhyming lines arranged 1–4, 2–5 and 3–6. The delayed rhymes, together with the enjambment after the third lines, make each stanza an uninterrupted unit. There is craft (in both senses) also in the use of 'headpiece' (seemingly colloquial but in fact archaic). Housman had a wide command of English 'on historical principles', as the Oxford English Dictionary was originally subtitled, and knew that the word had been used in the sense of 'brain' since at least the early seventeenth century. Its appearance here lulls the reader into thinking the poem a simple bucolic lament – but instead, step by step, it rises in the last four lines to a perfectly composed rhetorical climax.

Housman achieves the same sort of effect by rather less elaborate means in 'Eight o'clock', the second (and far the stronger) of a pair of poems on men awaiting execution:

XV

He stood and heard the steeple
 Sprinkle the quarters on the morning town.
One, two, three, four, to market-place and people
 It tossed them down.

Strapped, noosed, nighing his hour,
 He stood and counted them and cursed his luck;
And then the clock collected in the tower
 Its strength, and struck.

In the printed version of *The Name and Nature of Poetry* Housman added a footnote on the art of versification in which he lists the main things that poets need to know, whether by learning or by instinct, including 'the presence in verse of silent and invisible feet, like rests in music' – exactly as in the last line of 'Eight o'clock'. He was no untutored genius warbling (in Milton's phrase) 'his native woodnotes wild'. Housman, from his vast reading of poetry, was as steeped in prosody as Milton himself, or Pope or Gray. It took great skill to hide the even greater skill with which he wrote.

6

From Beyond the Grave

The strain of working on the Leslie Stephen lecture and delivering it exhausted Housman. He started to feel ill and depressed, and was in fact suffering from the early stages of heart disease, which made breathing difficult when he lay down. The only way he could sleep was by sitting up in bed, and even then he was constantly woken by breathlessness.

Ill health did not stop him working, and he continued his programme of lectures and the duties of supervision that came with the Trinity fellowship. His correspondence had grown over the years. There were constant letters from admirers asking questions about his poetry, requests for permission to reprint poems, begging letters – all in addition to correspondence with fellow scholars on classical subjects. He was scrupulous in answering, and nearly always kind.

One matter that concerned Housman in these years was the future of his poems. There had already been suggestions for combining *A Shropshire Lad* and *Last Poems* into a single volume. He resisted the idea as silly. They were separate books, distinct in character. In each of them he had been at pains to avoid repetition of ideas and (as far as possible) content. Combining them, he judged, would be to produce an incoherent and indigestible volume.

There was also the question of poems he had omitted from the two books. Some he had left out as not good enough, but far more had been rejected because there were too many others in the same form or metre, or simply to keep the extent of the books within the narrow bounds he set himself, or because they were too private – for instance 'Oh who is that young sinner?' and 'Because I liked you better'. Poems that were good enough he did not want wasted, but nothing incomplete or below standard should appear. There was no question of departing from his resolve to publish no more himself, but if his wishes were to be followed, he needed a literary executor to select and arrange the poems and see them through the press. For the task he chose his brother Laurence, a fellow poet who had been helpful with *Last Poems*. Moreover, Laurence was openly sympathetic to the plight of homosexuals (and was one himself), and was therefore probably a better judge of the most personal poems. He was accordingly asked to go through Housman's notebooks, select what was good enough to print, and destroy anything incomplete or not up to standard.

A little less than three years after *The Name and Nature of Poetry* Housman died. Well organised as always, he had written a poem to be sung as a hymn at his funeral (and given a copy to the Dean of Trinity for use when needed). He was no Christian himself ('I became a deist at thirteen and an atheist at twenty-one', he told an enquirer in 1933), and had set himself the difficult task of producing something without pretence of faith but acceptable in an Anglican service. The result was three short verses in which he reverts to deism but uses the language of English hymns:

> O thou that from thy mansion
>> Through time and place to roam,
> Dost send abroad thy children,
>> And then dost call them home,
>
> That men and tribes and nations
>> And all thy hand hath made
> May shelter them from sunshine
>> In thine eternal shade:
>
> We now to peace and darkness
>> And earth and thee restore
> Thy creature whom thou madest
>> And wilt cast forth no more.

(*More Poems*, XLVII)

It is bland on the surface, but not in implication. The god addressed (in the conventional form as 'thou') sends out – or 'casts forth' – humans to wander the earth, and then calls them home to 'peace and darkness'. This is no Christian God, there is no praise, no mention of Christ, no triumph over death, no eternal plan for mankind. All that remains is a brief and pointless spell of exile from non-existence. It is Housman at his starkest.

Laurence, as well as being Housman's literary executor, inherited his literary rights, and he made the most of them. Less than six months after his brother's death, he published a book of forty-nine pieces under the title *More Poems*. In 1937 he produced a memoir, *A. E. H.*, containing a further eighteen poems (known as *Additional Poems*) as well as light verse and a selection of letters; and two years later, in outright defiance of his instructions, but for the convenience of readers and his own profit, he authorised the issue of Housman's *Collected Poems*, which added a further five poems and three translations of odes from Greek tragedy.

The posthumous selections include many of Housman's most memorable poems. Laurence who took the advice of three of Housman's Cambridge colleagues in assembling the contents of *More Poems*, did his work well. Feeling that it was too soon to print the poems about Jackson, he omitted them from the book, but in 1937 printed them, together with a handful of others, as *Additional Poems*. They tell the story simply and poignantly.

VII

He would not stay for me; and who can wonder?
　He would not stay for me to stand and gaze.
I shook his hand and tore my heart asunder
　And went with half my life about my ways.

Brief as it is, it is a complete poem. Housman may have thought it a fragment – he printed nothing so short in either of his own books – but could anything more have been said? As he presumably did not revise it, its present form may not represent his definite intention for it, but he was careful with his commas, and their absence from the two last lines, is likely to be deliberate – and eloquent.

The piece in *Additional Poems* that precedes it does not seem to be a draft at all. Housman habitually used the same rhyme scheme in successive verses and may have been dissatisfied with it for failing to pass that test. The first verse is rhymed like Fitzgerald's *Rubaiyát of Omar Khayyám* (though the indentation differs); the second is a regular quatrain. The lines are decasyllabic throughout, but achieve the same sort of musicality as Tennyson's blank verse lyric 'Tears, idle tears', and any disruption from the change in rhyme pattern is muted by the double repetition of the first line as a refrain, which unifies the poem by maintaining the same rhyme-sound throughout:

Ask me no more, for fear I should reply;
   Others have held their tongues, and so can I;
Hundreds have died, and told no tale before;
   Ask me no more, for fear I should reply—

How one was true and one was clean of stain
   And one was braver than the heavens are high,
And one was fond of me; and all are slain.
   Ask me no more, for fear I should reply.

If this is a draft, it has a high degree of finish in the details – for example, the absence of punctuation from line 5 and the comma at the end of line 6, setting 'And one was fond of me' apart from the three others, to be followed by the dead finality of the full stop after 'slain'.

More Poems (though this is not the conventional view) contains as many of Housman's best poems as either *A Shropshire Lad* or *Last Poems*. In addition to 'Because I liked you better' (XXXI), and the beautiful 'Parta Quies' (XLVIII), with which the book ends, it contains poems of all the types in which Housman excelled. There is the noble translation from Horace, opening:

V

Diffugere nives

The snows are fled away, leaves on the shaws
   And grasses in the mead renew their birth,
The river to the river-bed withdraws,
   And altered is the fashion of the earth.

The Nymphs and Graces three put off their fear
   And unapparelled in the woodland play.
The swift hour and the brief prime of the year
   Say to the soul, *Thou wast not born for aye* …

This is followed by a song (not labelled as one, but the closest Housman came to writing words as though intended for music):

I to my perils
   Of cheat and charmer
   Came clad in armour
      By stars benign.
Hope lies to mortals
   And most believe her,
   But man's deceiver
      Was never mine.

The thoughts of others
   Were light and fleeting,
   Of lovers' meeting
      Or luck or fame.
Mine were of trouble,
   And mine were steady,
   So I was ready
      When trouble came.

There is metrical virtuosity here. The short iambic lines, with their free-floating stresses, feminine endings and enjambments, the constantly shifting vowel sounds held in check only by the demands of rhyme – all these keep the movement swift and light.

Housman seems to come close to the same effect in the opening of 'Tarry, delight', but the poem is dark: it recalls Ovid's tragic tale of Hero and her lover Leander, drowned as he swims over the stormy Hellespont after a brief hour of happiness in her arms:

XV

Tarry, delight, so seldom met,
   So sure to perish, tarry still;
Forbear to cease or languish yet,
   Though soon you must and will.

By Sestos town, in Hero's tower,
   On Hero's heart Leander lies;
The signal torch has burned its hour
   And sputters as it dies.

> Beneath him, in the nighted firth,
>> Between two continents complain
> The seas he swam from earth to earth
>> And he must swim again.

All is understatement here. We are a thousand miles, in poetic art as well as geography, from the blundering drunks at Ludlow. Housman has found his lyric voice ('Rarely, rarely comest thou, spirit of delight'), and there is perfect precision, economy and power of suggestion in the words. Where he has 'On Hero's heart', a poorer poet would have written the obvious but less expressive (because merely physical) 'breast'; 'sputters as it dies' adds menace to 'the nighted firth', the treacherous waters that 'between two continents complain' ('nighted' now for want of Hero's beacon). Leander must swim 'from earth to earth', from Europe to Asia, and the final 'again' warns that it will be to his death. The metre adds its own touch to the feeling of ill fortune close at hand: each verse has three lines of eight syllables, followed by a shorter six-syllable line, a dying fall.

'Tarry delight' is one of the poems Housman began at about the time of *A Shropshire Lad* but left incomplete till early April 1922 when he was collecting the material for *Last Poems*. There is no obvious explanation for his decision to leave it out. Possibly he was dissatisfied with the third and fourth lines, which may be 'fillers'. Certainly there is nothing else resembling it in *Last Poems*, and its omission more probably results simply from Housman's self-imposed limit of forty-one poems.

Another of the pieces intended for *Last Poems* but not chosen in the end is:

> The rainy Pleiads wester,
>> Orion plunges prone,
> The stroke of midnight ceases,
>> And I lie down alone.

> The rainy Pleiads wester
>> And seek beyond the sea
> The head that I shall dream of,
>> And 'twill not dream of me.

(More Poems, XI)

Here there is no mystery in Housman's decision. The poem is his second attempt at embroidering (and perhaps completing) Sappho's famous fragment (or poem? If it is only a fragment, it leaves one wondering what more could have followed): 'The moon has set, the Pleiads also; midnight is here and gone, and I sleep alone.' His first variant appears as *More Poems*, x. Its successor (the poem above) repeats the line but is otherwise completely different, though still openly derived from Sappho. Finally Housman wrote a third version, 'The half-moon westers low, my love', and that is the one that appears as *Last Poems*, XXVI – and is the furthest removed from its Greek starting-point. To read the three poems in succession is to see Housman first paring down the slightly rhetorical original attempt, only to romanticise the restrained version printed here, one near in spirit to the Greek, to a romantic ballad, almost in the manner of Burns, ending:

> I know not if it rains, my love,
>   In the land where you do lie;
> And oh, so sound you sleep, my love,
>   You know no more than I.

(There is another glimpse of his thoughts on style in a letter to one of the friends he consulted about *Last Poems*, cheerfully answering an objection to the seeming artificiality of 'you do lie': it 'is not really for metre's sake, but an imitation, false I daresay, of the ballads which I do imitate'.)

Although Housman had avoided publishing single-stanza pieces, Laurence included three in *More Poems* (and six more in *Additional Poems*). He was right to do so. Of the ones in *More Poems*, two are clearly complete and can never have been intended to say anything further; the other, which follows here, though probably no more than a fragment of a narrative poem, perhaps autobiographical, tells the whole story in its four lines.

> He, standing hushed, a pace or two apart,
>   Among the bluebells of the listless plain,
> Thinks, and remembers how he cleansed his heart
>   And washed his hands in innocence in vain.

(More Poems, XXVIII)

The two other short poems can never have been intended as part of anything else.

> To stand up straight and tread the turning mill,
> To lie flat and know nothing and be still,
> Are the two trades of man; and which is worse
> I know not, but I know that both are ill.   (*More Poems*, XXVII)

Like the first stanza of 'Ask me no more', this is in the *Omar Khayyám* verse form, but it resembles the other poem in no other way. 'Ask me no more' is pure melody; 'To stand up straight' is nearly prose in comparison, but there is more than mere rhyme and alliteration to make it a poem. The treadmill metaphor for life; the three commonplace phrases in the second line to convey the bleak emptiness of death; the use of 'trades' (with the Victorian self-styled gentleman's scorn for the shopkeeper) for all that humans can achieve in life and all they may hope to find beyond: these combine to confer nobility on the acceptance that though existence may be pointless, one may still 'stand up straight' honourably and make what one can of the labour at the mill – like Samson 'at the mill with slaves'.

Housman always detested the senseless waste of young lives in war. It was his misfortune in his early years to live through a period of almost constant frontier fighting and rebellions in the Empire, accompanied by two wars in South Africa and followed by the unsurpassed horror of the First World War, commemorated in his 'Epitaph on an Army of Mercenaries'. Years earlier he had written a similar but less rhetorical poem closer to the form of the Greek epitaph, in which the buried dead are imagined speaking from the tomb:

> Here dead lie we because we did not choose
>   To live and shame the land from which we sprung.
> Life, to be sure, is nothing much to lose;
>   But young men think it is, and we were young.

> (*More Poems*, XXXVI)

It is a poem that may stand as Housman's memorial. The classical form, the irony, the understatement, the honour paid to courage, the pity for men cheated of life's few pleasures: these are all marks of the poet and the man alike.

Metrical composition is no longer seriously studied as it once was, and few poets now have the acute awareness, possessed by many earlier writers, of sound and its power by patterning and repetition to evoke emotion as harmonic progressions do in music. Housman acquired it, like most of his predecessors, from learning the discipline of writing verse in Greek and Latin at an early age. There can be few living now that possess half his knowledge of the vocabulary of English, of metres, of the resolution and inversion of feet, the colour of every vowel and diphthong, the use of rhyme, assonance and alliteration to unify the stanza, the effect of end-stopping and enjambment, of syllabic length and punctuation in regulating the speed of lines. Such knowledge does not make a poet, but its constant use helps those born with the divine spark. There have been fine poets, some great poets, since Housman, but few with so good a claim to be honoured as a lord of language.

Bibliography

Housman's poetry

A Shropshire Lad, London, 1896

Last Poems, London, 1922

More Poems, London, 1936

Collected Poems, London, 1939

The Manuscript Poems of A. E. Housman, edited by
    Tom Burns Haber, Oxford, 1955

The Poems of A. E. Housman, edited by Archie Burnett,
    Oxford, 1997

Biography and letters

A. S. F. Gow, *A. E. Housman: A Sketch*, Cambridge, 1936

Laurence Housman, *A. E. H.: Some Poems, Some Letters and
    a Personal Memoir by his Brother*, London, 1937

Percy Withers, *A Buried Life: Personal Recollections of
    A. E. Housman*, London, 1940

Grant Richards, *Housman 1897–1936*, Oxford, 1941

Richard Perceval Graves, *A. E. Housman: The Scholar-Poet*,
    London, 1979

The Letters of A. E. Housman, edited by Archie Burnett,
    Oxford, 2007